Chester, UK Travel Guide 2024

Delve into the past and present of Chester's Architectural Splendors.

Zayyan Alee

Copyright © 2023 Zayyan Alee

All rights reserved. No part of this publication may be reproduced, distributed, or transmitted in any form or by any means, including photocopying, recording, or other electronic or mechanical methods, without the prior written permission of the copyright owner.

Table of Content

Introduction 6

About Chester 8

Geography of Chester 9

History 10

Map of UK 12

Map of Chester 13

Why do people travel to Chester 14

Chester City photo highlight 16

Most popular type of Tourism in Chester 17

Plan your visit to Chester 19

    Getting to Chester 19

How to get to Chester from London 23

When is the best season to go to Chester 25

How long do i need to plan on being in Chester 26

How can I navigate Chester 27

Accommodations in Chester 29

    Budget friendly accommodations 30

Getting around/ Transportation system 33
- On foot and by bike 35
- By rail and car 39
- Public restrooms 41
- Accessible route for all 42

Itineraries 43
- Chester in 3days 43
  - Day 1: Historical Immersion 43
  - Day 2: Cultural Immersion 44
  - Day 3: Nature and Relaxation 45
- Where to eat 46
  - Day 1: Historical Exploration 46
  - Day 2: Cultural Immersion 46
  - Day 3: Nature and Relaxation 46

Tips for visiting Chester 48

Health considerations 51
- Security and safety 53

Attractions places to visit and things to do 57

Tours and experience in chester 60

FAQs 64

Top5 Attraction in Chester 67

Where to eat in Chester 69

Where to shop in Chester 72

Chester travel final thought 75

Introduction

Welcome to the city of Chester, where an amalgamation of historical resonance and contemporary vibrancy characterizes its quaint cobblestone streets. Situated along the picturesque River Dee, Chester epitomizes a harmonious coexistence of medieval relics, verdant landscapes, and a dynamic cultural milieu. This comprehensive guide serves as a conduit for delving into the city's rich tapestry, offering insights into its ancient walls and bustling thoroughfares.

Immerse oneself in the intricate historical narrative, observing the iconic medieval Rows and meticulously preserved Roman walls that stand as testament to the passage of centuries. Beyond the veneer of antiquity, Chester reveals itself as a living entity, pulsating with cultural offerings, gastronomic indulgences, and a hospitable atmosphere that beckons exploration.

Catering to diverse interests, be it historical enthusiasts fascinated by architectural marvels, gastronomes eager to partake in local culinary experiences, or leisure seekers desiring a serene riverside escape, Chester guarantees a distinctive sojourn. This guide endeavours to navigate through the essence of the city, where each street corner narrates a unique tale and every landmark mirrors the timeless allure defining Chester. Embark on this academic exploration, inviting you to unravel the concealed facets, delectations, and captivating charm inherent to this historical gem on the banks of the River Dee.

About Chester

Chester, situated on the banks of the River Dee in northwest England, is a compelling fusion of historical resonance and contemporary dynamism. Evident in its meticulously conserved Roman walls and iconic Rows, the city encapsulates a rich medieval heritage. Its cultural vibrancy, diverse gastronomic offerings, and picturesque landscapes render it an engaging prospect for discerning travelers. Chester beckons exploration of its historical troves, encompassing landmarks such as the esteemed Chester Cathedral and the Roman Amphitheatre, all within an ambiance characterized by affability and hospitality.

Geography of Chester

Chester is situated in the north western region of England, strategically positioned along the banks of the River Dee. The city features a predominantly level topography, enhancing its historical aesthetic and facilitating ease of navigation. The River Dee, flowing adjacent to Chester, not only enhances the city's picturesque setting but also holds historical significance in its development.

Additionally, Chester is distinguished by its meticulously preserved Roman walls, encompassing a substantial portion of the city's central area. These ancient fortifications serve as a tangible testament to the city's historical eminence and contribute significantly to its distinct geographical attributes.

The surrounding environs exhibit a juxtaposition of urban and rural landscapes, presenting a diverse backdrop conducive to both historical exploration and contemporary activities. In summation, Chester's geographical configuration, marked by the river, historic walls, and a harmonious blend of urban and natural elements, underscores its appeal as a multifaceted and engaging locale.

History

Chester boasts a historical tapestry spanning more than two millennia, with its origins traced back to its establishment as a Roman fort in AD 79, recognized as Deva Victrix. A pivotal player in Roman Britain, Chester's enduring Roman heritage is evident in the remarkably preserved walls and amphitheatre.

Transitioning into the medieval epoch, Chester flourished as a thriving market town and a hub of commerce. The venerable Chester Cathedral, erected in 1093, stands as an architectural testament to the city's ecclesiastical prominence during this period.

The annals of Chester's history are marked by nuanced shifts in political and social dynamics, notably witnessed during the English Civil War in the 17th century. The distinctive Tudor-style architecture, exemplified in structures like The Rows, reflects the enduring medieval influence on the city's aesthetic.

Continuously evolving, Chester seamlessly integrates its historical legacy with contemporary amenities, forming a dynamic urban landscape. The tangible echoes of its multifaceted history resonate through the city's streets, walls, and structures, encapsulating centuries of transformative change and cultural progression.

Map of UK

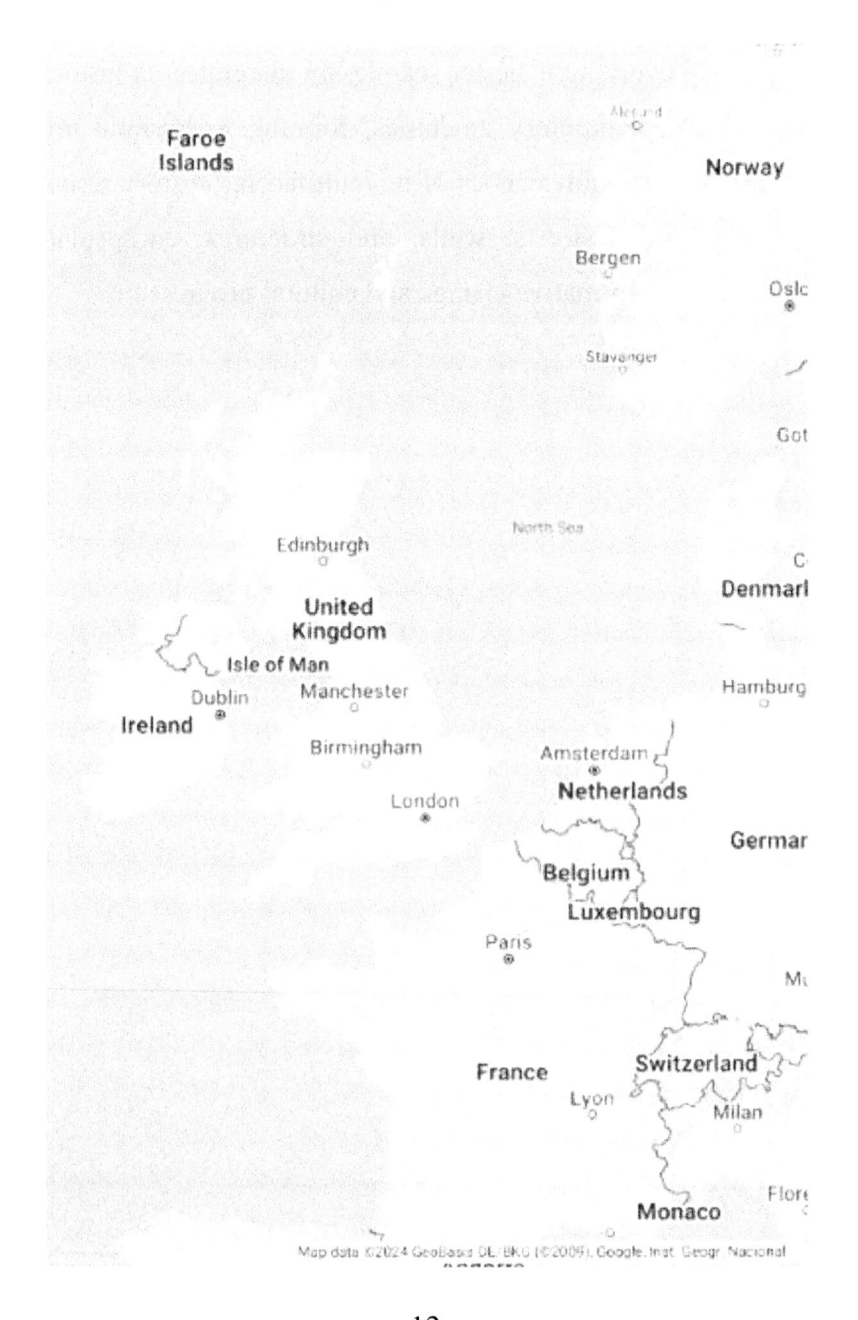

Map of Chester

Why do people travel to Chester

The magnetic appeal of Chester as a destination for travelers is multifaceted, encompassing various factors:

1. Historical Allure: Chester's profound historical resonance, epitomized by meticulously maintained Roman walls, medieval architectural treasures, and the venerable Chester Cathedral, entices aficionados of historical narratives seeking to immerse themselves in the city's past.

2. Architectural Distinctiveness: The city's distinctive black-and-white Tudor-style structures, prominently featured in The Rows, hold a particular fascination for those with an appreciation for unique and aesthetically pleasing architectural expressions.

3. Cultural Engagement: Chester's vibrant cultural milieu, manifest through museums, galleries, and theaters, provides an avenue for visitors to actively participate in intellectual and artistic endeavors.

4. Scenic Environs: Positioned along the River Dee and encompassed by idyllic countryside, Chester offers a serene escape for nature enthusiasts and outdoor aficionados.

5. Shopping and Gastronomy: The city's reputation for charming shops, markets, and diverse dining establishments lures individuals seeking a blend of historic ambiance and contemporary amenities.

6. Festive Atmosphere: Chester's calendar of events and festivals adds a dynamic dimension, attracting those desiring cultural immersion and participation in celebratory occasions.

7. Family-Oriented Appeal: The city's family-friendly offerings, such as the renowned Chester Zoo and activities catering to all age groups, position it as an attractive destination for travelers with children.

8. Walled City Experience: The meticulously preserved Roman walls provide visitors with the opportunity to traverse the historic city walls, offering panoramic vistas and a palpable sense of temporal transition.

In summation, Chester's allure for travelers resides in its synthesis of historical depth, cultural richness, natural aesthetics, and contemporary conveniences, rendering it a compelling destination for a diverse spectrum of interests and inclinations.

Chester City photo highlight

Most popular type of Tourism in Chester

Chester exhibits a multifaceted appeal to tourists, with distinct emphases on various thematic interests:

1. **Historical Tourism:** The city's profound historical narrative, articulated through its well-preserved Roman walls, medieval architectural heritage, and significant landmarks, positions it as a focal point for aficionados seeking immersion in antiquity.

2. **Cultural Tourism:** Chester's dynamic cultural landscape, encompassing museums, galleries, and theaters, caters to individuals with a proclivity for intellectual and artistic engagement.

3. **Architectural Tourism:** The unique black-and-white Tudor-style structures, prominently featured in The Rows, attract architectural enthusiasts keen on exploring and appreciating distinctive urban structures.

4. **Nature and Scenic Tourism:** Chester's picturesque locale along the River Dee, coupled with the surrounding countryside, establishes it as an enticing destination for those inclined towards natural aesthetics and outdoor pursuits.

5. **Family Tourism:** The family-friendly amenities, exemplified by the renowned Chester Zoo and activities

tailored for children, position Chester as an appealing choice for family-oriented travel.

6. **Shopping Tourism:** The city's array of charming shops, markets, and diverse shopping opportunities beckons those interested in retail experiences and the exploration of locally distinctive products.

7. **Event and Festival Tourism:** Chester's annual calendar of events and festivals serves as a draw for individuals seeking to partake in cultural celebrations and festive atmospheres.

8. **Culinary Tourism:** The diverse culinary landscape, encompassing traditional and contemporary options, positions Chester as an attractive destination for those with an interest in gastronomic exploration.

In summation, Chester's allure to tourists is underscored by a rich tapestry of historical, cultural, and architectural elements, reflecting a nuanced interplay of thematic attractions that contribute to its popularity among diverse traveler preferences.

Plan your visit to Chester

Planning your visit to Chester involves considering key aspects to make the most of your experience:

Getting to Chester

Accessing Chester is facilitated through a range of transportation modalities, offering convenience and flexibility:

1. Rail Transportation:

Chester is equipped with a centrally situated railway station, fostering connectivity to major urban centers such as London, Manchester, and Liverpool. The station's proximity to key attractions renders it a viable and accessible transit point.

2. Automobile Travel:

For those opting for vehicular transport, Chester is strategically situated along prominent motorways, including the M53 and M56. The city provides parking facilities, supplemented by park-and-ride alternatives for individuals seeking to circumvent city center traffic.

3. Air Travel:

Major airports, namely Manchester Airport and Liverpool John Lennon Airport, serve as proximate points of entry. Efficient rail, bus, taxi, and car rental services link these airports to Chester, ensuring diverse transport options for incoming travelers.

4. Bus Commute:

National and regional bus services afford a cost-effective means of transit to and from Chester, with the central bus station conveniently located in close proximity to the railway station.

5. Maritime Arrival:

An alternative and distinctive mode of arrival involves navigating the River Dee via boat. Boat tours are available, and some visitors choose to moor their narrow boats within the city, providing an unconventional yet scenic entrance.

Upon arrival in Chester, the city's pedestrian-friendly layout facilitates on-foot exploration, with local bus services and taxis offering supplementary transit alternatives within the urban landscape. The choice of transportation can be tailored to individual preferences and logistical considerations.

Visa and entry requirements

As of the most recent information available in January 2022, the particulars of visa and entry requirements are subject to potential revisions, emphasizing the necessity of consulting the latest data prior to planning a visit to Chester. While providing broad guidelines, it is imperative to recognize that the specifics may vary contingent upon one's nationality and other pertinent factors.

1. European Union (EU) Citizens:

EU citizens typically do not necessitate a visa for entry into the UK, including Chester. Adherence to this provision mandates possession of a valid passport or a national ID card.

2. Non-EU Citizens:

Individuals not hailing from EU member states may be obligated to obtain a visa for entry into the UK. The category of visa requisite is contingent upon the purpose and duration of the visit. Precision in understanding these requisites can be obtained by referring to the official website of the UK government or by contacting the British embassy or consulate pertinent to one's nation of origin.

3. Visitor Visa:

For brief sojourns, a Standard Visitor Visa may be sought, catering to purposes such as tourism, business, or familial visits. Adhering to eligibility criteria and initiating the application process well in advance of the intended travel date is advised.

4. Electronic Travel Authorization (ETA):

Certain nationals may qualify for the Electronic Travel Authorization (ETA) system, affording visa-free travel for abbreviated stays. Preliminary verification of eligibility and the submission of an online application are prerequisites for this facilitative measure.

5. Transit Passengers:

For individuals transiting through the UK, consideration should be given to the possible requisites for a Direct Airside Transit Visa (DATV) or a Visitor in Transit Visa. The specific mandates hinge on the intricacies of one's travel arrangements.

6. COVID-19 Entry Restrictions:

The on-going global COVID-19 pandemic has introduced additional entry requirements, encompassing health declarations, mandatory testing, and quarantine protocols. Staying abreast of the latest developments in COVID-19 travel guidelines is imperative, with compliance to any extant restrictions being paramount.

7. Travel Insurance:

The acquisition of comprehensive travel insurance is recommended, covering potential health exigencies and unforeseen disruptions to travel plans. Certain visa categories may mandate the provision of evidence of insurance coverage.

A steadfast recommendation is to diligently ascertain the prevailing visa and entry stipulations from authoritative government sources or liaise directly with the relevant embassy or consulate. Furthermore, recognition should be accorded to the potential evolution of entry policies, particularly in response to public health considerations.

How to get to Chester from London

For travellers seeking to traverse the distance from London to Chester, several modalities present themselves:

1. Train:

Direct railway services originating from London Euston and terminating in Chester offer a streamlined and expeditious mode of transportation, boasting a travel time of approximately 2 hours. Schedules and ticket reservations can be accessed and secured through the official National Rail website or relevant train operators.

2. Automobile:

Opting for a personal vehicle entails navigating the northbound M6 motorway from London to reach Chester. The duration of this journey, typically around 4 hours, is contingent upon traffic conditions and the selected route. Ample parking facilities, inclusive of city center car parks, are available in Chester.

3. Bus:

National Express and other bus service providers furnish transportation options departing from London Victoria Coach Station to Chester. The temporal span of this journey, ranging from 4 to 5 hours, hinges on route particulars and potential stops. Online perusal of bus schedules and ticket procurement can be executed through the respective bus company's official website.

4. Aviation:

While Chester lacks a direct airport, travelers can consider aerial transportation from London to proximate airports, such as Manchester Airport or Liverpool John Lennon Airport. Subsequently, the continuation of the journey to Chester can be realized via train or other local modes of transit.

Irrespective of the chosen mode of conveyance, prudent consideration of schedules, advance ticket reservations, and the alignment of travel preferences with factors like duration and convenience is advisable. The railway option, acknowledged for its celerity and popularity, emerges as a prevalent choice for those journeying from London to Chester.

When is the best season to go to Chester

Optimal seasons for visiting Chester generally align with spring (April to June) and autumn (September to October). During these periods, the climate is temperate, and the cityscape is embellished with either blossoming flowers in spring or the vibrant hues of autumn foliage. Summer (July to August) is viable as well, providing warmer temperatures, although it tends to be more crowded with tourists. Winter (December to February) entails cooler weather, and while the festive ambiance adds allure, certain outdoor attractions may operate on reduced schedules. The selection of an ideal season is contingent upon individual preferences, with spring and autumn standing out for a harmonious blend of agreeable weather conditions and a more subdued tourist presence.

How long do i need to plan on being in Chester

The optimal duration for a vacation in Chester is contingent upon individual inclinations and the scope of intended exploration. A comprehensive visit typically encompasses a span of 2 to 3 days, affording ample time for the thorough examination of historical landmarks, such as the Roman walls and Chester Cathedral, as well as the enjoyment of the distinctive shopping experience found in The Rows. This timeframe also facilitates the appreciation of cultural attractions, culinary indulgences, and the potential inclusion of a leisurely boat excursion along the River Dee. However, individuals with a predilection for a more unhurried itinerary or an inclination to explore the encompassing countryside may elect to extend their stay. The determination of an optimal duration is fundamentally contingent upon the particular proclivities of the visitor and the depth of engagement sought within the historical and cultural milieu of Chester.

How can I navigate Chester

Efficiently navigating the city of Chester is facilitated by its compact dimensions and well-preserved historical layout. The following recommendations ensure a seamless and enjoyable exploration:

1. Pedestrian Exploration:

Due to the city's pedestrian-friendly design, traversing Chester on foot is highly recommended. This allows for a leisurely exploration of landmarks like the Rows and the city walls.

2. Utilization of City Walls:

The Roman walls encircling the city serve not only as historical artifacts but also as navigational aids, offering panoramic vistas and a unique perspective of Chester.

3. Cartographic Resources and Signage:

Access maps from the Visitor Information Centre or utilize digital mapping tools for orientation. Clear signage and information boards strategically placed throughout the city further enhance navigation.

4. Landmark Utilization:

Prominent landmarks such as Chester Cathedral, the Eastgate Clock, and the Rows can be employed as reference points, aiding in spatial orientation.

5. Guided Tour Consideration:

Opting for a guided walking tour is a viable strategy for effective navigation. Knowledgeable guides not only elucidate historical nuances but also highlight key points of interest.

6. Public Transportation Inclusion:

Chester's well-established bus network provides an additional mode of transportation for those inclined towards public transit, linking various city locales and adjacent areas.

7. River Dee Promenade:

The scenic River Dee contributes to navigation with picturesque walking paths along its banks. Boat tours on the river offer an alternative and captivating view of the city.

8. Bicycle Rental Option:

For an eco-friendly exploration, bicycle rentals are available. This mode of transportation enables visitors to cover more ground while enjoying the city and its environs.

The navigational attributes of Chester, marked by walk able streets, distinctive landmarks, and historical allure, not only facilitate practical orientation but also contribute substantively to the overall allure of the city.

Accommodations in Chester

Lodging options in Chester are diverse, catering to a spectrum of preferences and encompassing a fusion of historical aesthetics and contemporary conveniences. These options include:

1. Historic Inns and Boutique Hotels:

Chester features a selection of historic inns and boutique hotels, situated either within the city centre or in close proximity, offering guests an immersive experience characterized by unique architectural elements and period-specific features.

2. Modern Hotels:

Several modern hotels, strategically positioned along the River Dee or in immediate proximity to key attractions, provide contemporary amenities, ensuring a comfortable and convenient sojourn.

3. Guesthouses and Bed and Breakfasts:

Quaint guesthouses and bed and breakfast establishments, nestled in charming residential locales, extend a personalized touch to lodging, fostering a homely ambiance and an opportunity for local engagement.

4. Self-Catering Apartments:

For those desiring heightened autonomy, self-catering apartments represent a flexible option. Equipped with kitchen facilities, these accommodations are conducive to extended stays.

5. Luxury Accommodations:

Chester is home to luxury hotels that deliver premium services, culinary excellence, and spa facilities, ensuring a lavish and indulgent experience for the discerning traveler.

6. Budget-Friendly Options:

Considerate of budget constraints, there exist affordable hotels, hostels, and economically viable chain accommodations, providing a balance between comfort and cost-effectiveness.

7. Rural Retreats:

In the encompassing countryside, one finds country hotels and bed and breakfast establishments, offering a serene retreat while affording convenient access to Chester's attractions.

Prudent pre-booking is advisable, particularly during peak seasons or noteworthy events. This array of lodging alternatives caters to the diverse preferences of visitors, accommodating those inclined toward historical immersion, contemporary amenities, or economically conscious choices.

Budget friendly accommodations

Chester provides a spectrum of accommodations that cater to budget-conscious travellers, enabling them to explore the city economically. These options encompass:

1. Economical Hotels:

Various budget hotels strategically positioned within or in proximity to the city center, afford reasonably priced rooms equipped with essential amenities. These lodgings are typically well-linked to public transportation and major points of interest.

2. Hostels:

Hostels present a cost-effective choice, featuring dormitory-style accommodations that resonate with budget-conscious individuals. Some hostels also offer private rooms, providing an additional layer of seclusion.

3. Chain Establishments:

Recognized budget-friendly hotel chains have established a presence in Chester, delivering reliable and economically viable lodging options accompanied by standard amenities.

4. Guesthouses and Bed and Breakfasts:

In residential enclaves, guesthouses and bed and breakfast establishments offer an intimate setting with an economical edge. Many of these lodgings include breakfast as part of the room rate.

5. Self-Catering Apartments:

For those desiring autonomy in culinary matters, self-catering apartments represent a thrifty alternative. Furnished with kitchen facilities, these lodgings facilitate meal preparation at the discretion of the guest.

Pre-emptive reservations are advisable to secure favourable rates, especially during peak periods or events. While tailored to budget considerations, these accommodations uphold a standard of comfort, enabling visitors to partake in the historical and cultural offerings of Chester without compromising on financial prudence.

Getting around/ Transportation system

Navigating Chester is facilitated by its compact scale and a well-coordinated transportation infrastructure. The primary modes of transportation encompass:

1. Pedestrian Exploration:

Chester's city center is meticulously designed for pedestrian traversal, affording individuals the opportunity to ambulate through streets, discover historical landmarks, and immerse themselves in the city's quaint ambiance.

2. City Walls:

The meticulously preserved Roman walls serve a dual purpose, bearing historical significance while concurrently providing an aesthetically pleasing pathway for pedestrians. The act of strolling along these walls offers an idiosyncratic viewpoint of Chester.

3. Public Bus Network:

Chester features an extensive bus network that seamlessly interlinks diverse areas within the city and its periphery. This mode of transportation, marked by affordability and accessibility, proves advantageous for both local and regional travel. The central bus station is strategically positioned in proximity to the railway station.

4. Taxicabs:

Taxis, easily procurable either on the street or via prearrangement, constitute a flexible and efficient means of transportation, particularly for shorter distances.

5. River Boat Tours:

Boat tours along the River Dee offer a picturesque and unhurried avenue for exploring the city. This mode of transportation not only imparts a distinct vantage point but also contributes to a leisurely exploration of Chester.

6. Cycling:

Chester embraces a bicycle-friendly environment, with designated paths and rental services catering to those inclined towards cycling as a mode of transportation. This presents an enjoyable and eco-conscious alternative.

7. Car Rental Services:

While the city center is designed for pedestrian use, the option of renting a car proves advantageous for venturing into the surrounding countryside or accessing attractions beyond the immediate urban confines. Numerous car rental agencies operate within Chester.

8. Rail Transport:

The centrally located train station connects Chester to major urban centres, rendering train travel an efficient option for those desiring exploration beyond the city's immediate environs.

Endowed with pedestrian-friendly avenues, diverse transportation modalities, and the intrinsic charm of its historical layout, Chester offers a practical and pleasurable landscape for navigation.

On foot and by bike

Engaging with Chester through pedestrian exploration and bicycling offers an intimate and environmentally conscious approach to experiencing the city's allure:

Pedestrian Exploration:

1. City Center Designed for Pedestrians:

Chester's urban core is thoughtfully crafted to accommodate pedestrians, featuring well-maintained thoroughfares, historic landmarks, and architecturally captivating structures. A leisurely promenade through the city enables a nuanced appreciation of its distinct character.

2. Traverse Along City Walls:

The Roman fortifications enveloping Chester provide an elevated and aesthetically pleasing promenade. Undertaking a walk atop the city walls not only imparts historical context but also affords panoramic vistas of Chester's topography.

3. Access to Historical Sites:

Many of Chester's historical gems, such as the Rows and Chester Cathedral, are conveniently reachable on foot. This mode of exploration allows for a detailed examination of the intricate facets of the city's historical tapestry.

Bicycling:

1. Promotion of Cycling Culture:

Chester actively fosters a cycling culture with designated paths, positioning itself as a city conducive to bicycling. Beyond its efficiency as a mode of transport, cycling embodies an active and sustainable means of traversing the urban landscape.

2. Scenic Cycling Routes Along River Dee:

Embarking on cycling routes along the River Dee introduces a scenic trajectory. Cyclists can relish riverside panoramas and a serene ambiance while navigating through allocated cycling zones.

3. Flexibility and Autonomy:

Bicycling affords a heightened degree of flexibility in surveying both the city and its outskirts. It empowers individuals with the freedom to cover extensive ground while immersing themselves in the outdoors.

4. Availability of Bicycle Rental Services:

Services providing bicycle rentals cater to residents and visitors alike in Chester. This amenity facilitates the experience of the city on two wheels without the encumbrance of ownership.

Whether on foot or astride a bicycle, Chester's compact urban design and commitment to pedestrian and cyclist infrastructure render it an ideal locale for those seeking an immersive and ecologically mindful approach to unraveling its rich historical tapestry and scenic environs.

By bus

Employing the bus transportation system in Chester constitutes a pragmatic and easily accessible mode of travel:

1. Extensive Transit Network:

Chester boasts a comprehensive bus network, intricately connecting diverse segments of the city and adjacent locales. This expansive network ensures widespread accessibility, catering to both residents and visitors.

2. Centralized Bus Terminal:

The central bus station, strategically positioned in close proximity to the railway station, functions as a pivotal hub for bus arrivals and departures. This centralized location enhances the overall convenience and navigability of the transit system.

3. Economical Transport Option:

Opting for bus travel within Chester is economically prudent, offering a budget-friendly alternative for individuals seeking to explore the city without incurring substantial transportation costs.

4. Regular Service Intervals:

The bus services in Chester maintain a consistent schedule, with buses operating at regular intervals throughout the day. This punctuality enhances the flexibility of travel planning for commuters.

5. Proximity to Key Attractions:

Buses in Chester are strategically routed to encompass prominent attractions, historical sites, and residential districts. This deliberate routing ensures convenient access for passengers to desired destinations within the city.

6. Intermodal Integration:

The bus system is intricately integrated with other modes of transportation, facilitating seamless transfers for individuals transitioning between buses, trains, or other transit alternatives.

7. Sustainability Considerations:

Opting for bus travel aligns with sustainable practices, contributing to the reduction of individual carbon footprints. This eco-friendly dimension enhances the appeal of bus transportation as a conscientious choice.

8. Accessible Information Resources:

Information services, including route maps and schedules, are readily accessible to assist passengers in planning their bus journeys. These informational resources play a crucial role in ensuring a well-informed and smooth travel experience.

Utilizing the bus transportation system in Chester emerges as a judicious and environmentally conscious means of navigating the city, characterized by its cost-effectiveness and expansive coverage of key urban areas.

By rail and car

Engaging with the city of Chester through the transportation modes of rail and car presents distinctive and efficient avenues for exploration:

By Rail:

1. Centrally Located Railway Station:

Chester is equipped with a centrally positioned railway station serving as a pivotal nexus for transportation. This station facilitates convenient ingress and egress to and from the city, establishing crucial connections to major urban centers.

2. Efficient Connectivity:

Rail travel stands out for its efficiency in connectivity, allowing passengers to expeditiously access neighboring regions or partake in day excursions to nearby attractions. The frequency of train services contributes to the accessibility and adaptability of travel options.

3. Regional and National Linkages:

Chester's railway infrastructure plays a vital role in establishing essential linkages at both regional and national levels. It provides a seamless means for residents and visitors to traverse diverse parts of the country.

4. Scenic Railway Journeys:

Train journeys often afford scenic vistas of the encompassing countryside. Beyond being a mere mode of conveyance, rail travel transforms into an opportunity for passengers to admire picturesque landscapes during transit.

By Car:

1. Accessible by Automobile:

Chester is accessible by road, boasting a well-interconnected network. Those opting for car travel enjoy the flexibility to navigate the city and its environs at their own rhythm.

2. Flexibility in Exploration:

The utilization of a car bestows exploratory flexibility, empowering travelers to venture beyond immediate city boundaries and delve into the scenic countryside. This autonomy proves particularly advantageous for those seeking bespoke itineraries.

3. Convenience for Day Excursions:

Cars facilitate day trips to nearby destinations and attractions that might not be as readily accessible by public transportation. This convenience enhances the practicality of exploring the broader region encompassing Chester.

4. Parking Facilities:

Chester provides designated parking facilities, including city center car parks, ensuring that individuals employing cars have accessible options for parking while engaging in foot exploration within the city.

5. Rural Exploration:

Car travel extends the spectrum of exploration to rural locales surrounding Chester, permitting a more exhaustive and personalized encounter with the broader geographical and cultural milieu.

Both rail and car transportation modalities offer distinct advantages, accommodating diverse preferences and travel objectives. While rail travel excels in efficiency and connectivity, car travel provides autonomy and the capacity to tailor one's journey within and outside the city confines.

Public restrooms

Public restroom facilities in Chester are strategically positioned throughout the city, meticulously placed to offer convenient accessibility for both residents and visitors. These amenities consistently uphold a level of cleanliness and are systematically tended to, contributing substantively to the favorable overall experience of individuals navigating the urban landscape. The deliberate placement of public restrooms in proximity to renowned attractions, parks, and commercial zones amplifies the accessibility and convenience for those engaged in exploration within Chester. Travelers can anticipate these facilities to adhere rigorously to established hygiene standards, presenting a dependable and essential option for restroom provisions during their sojourn in the city.

Accessible route for all

Chester exemplifies a commitment to inclusivity through the provision of accessible routes tailored to accommodate diverse mobility needs. These inclusive pathways incorporate meticulously maintained walkways, ramps, and tactile indicators, facilitating seamless navigation for individuals facing challenges related to mobility or wheelchair use. Public spaces, attractions, and amenities adhere to stringent accessibility standards, creating an environment wherein individuals of varying physical abilities can partake in and appreciate the city's offerings. This dedication to inclusivity enhances the overall experiential quality, establishing Chester as an inviting and accessible destination for a broad spectrum of individuals.

Itineraries

Devising curated itineraries in Chester offers a diverse spectrum of possibilities, ensuring a comprehensive exploration of the city's historical, cultural, and scenic facets. The following are proposed itineraries tailored to distinct interests:

Chester in 3days

Optimize your vacation in Chester with a meticulously devised three-day itinerary that intricately engages with the city's historical, cultural, and scenic tapestry.

Day 1: Historical Immersion

1. Morning:
- Commence your day at Chester Cathedral, where the intricate architecture and historical resonance unfold.
- Traverse the medieval Rows, embodying a distinctive shopping experience.

2. Afternoon:
- Proceed to Chester Castle and its medieval keep, delving into the city's military heritage.
- Partake in a leisurely luncheon at a charming establishment within the city center.

3. Evening:

- Embark on a contemplative stroll atop the impeccably preserved city walls, capturing expansive panoramas.
- Contribute to your historical understanding with an evening guided ghost tour.

Day 2: Cultural Immersion

1. Morning:

- Inaugurate the day at the Chester Art Centre, where contemporary and local artistic expressions converge.
- Immerse in the historical narrative at the Grosvenor Museum.

2. Afternoon:

- Immerse yourself in a performance or exhibition at the Storyhouse, Chester's cultural nucleus.
- Partake in a cultural luncheon at a restaurant nestled within the artistic district.

3. Evening:

- Culminate your day with a gastronomic experience at one of Chester's distinguished fine dining establishments, marrying culinary excellence with cultural nuances.

Day 3: Nature and Relaxation

1. Morning:

- Embark on a contemplative promenade along the River Dee, engaging with the natural allure.
- Seek solace in Grosvenor Park, an oasis of tranquility amidst verdant surroundings.

2. Afternoon:

- Opt for a scenic boat tour on the River Dee, indulging in a leisurely and picturesque interlude.
- Savor a relaxed luncheon at a café nestled along the riverside.

3. Evening:

- Conclude your day with an idyllic visit to the Roman Gardens, appreciating the serene atmosphere and the ethereal hues of the sunset.

This meticulously curated three-day itinerary endeavors to provide a comprehensive encounter with Chester, unraveling its historical depths, embracing its cultural vitality, and affording moments of repose amidst its scenic landscapes. Flexibility for personalization is encouraged based on individual preferences and the temporal context of the visit.

Where to eat

In the course of your explorations in Chester, consider the following dining venues to complement your itineraries:

Day 1: Historical Exploration

- Lunch: Select an establishment in the city center, preferably situated around Eastgate Street or Watergate Street, to indulge in a gastronomic experience amidst historical environs.
- Dinner: For the evening repast, peruse restaurants along Bridge Street, providing a synthesis of historical ambiance and contemporary culinary offerings.

Day 2: Cultural Immersion

- Lunch:Opt for a restaurant within the artistic district, proximate to the Storyhouse or the Chester Art Centre, to immerse in a culturally resonant luncheon experience.
- Dinner: Choose a fine dining establishment, situated, for instance, near St Werburgh Street, to complement the cultural facets of the day.

Day 3: Nature and Relaxation

- Lunch: Partake in a languid riverside luncheon at a café along the River Dee, offering panoramic vistas.

- Dinner: Conclude your day with an evening meal at a restaurant boasting outdoor seating, potentially in the vicinity of the Roman Gardens, affording a tranquil and atmospheric milieu.

These culinary recommendations are adaptable contingent upon individual inclinations and dietary considerations. Chester's diverse gastronomic landscape contributes a flavourful dimension to your holistic experience within the city.

Tips for visiting Chester

Enhance the efficacy of your visit to Chester with the following judicious recommendations:

1. In-depth Historical Exploration:
- **Tip:** Optimize your historical immersion by availing yourself of guided tours or utilizing audio guides at pivotal sites like Chester Cathedral and Chester Castle, thereby fostering a profound comprehension of the city's extensive historical tapestry.

2. Leisurely Stroll along City Walls:
- **Tip:** Commence a contemplative perambulation along the meticulously preserved city walls, ideally initiating this endeavor early to partake in a more serene ambulation and to behold panoramic vistas of Chester.

3. Gastronomic Inquiry:
- **Tip:** Undertake a gastronomic odyssey by exploring Chester's diverse culinary milieu. Sample indigenous delicacies such as Cheshire cheese and Chester Pudding, and frequent historic markets for a firsthand encounter with fresh, locally-sourced produce.

4. River Dee Nautical Exploration:
- **Tip:** Harness the opportunity to engage with Chester's scenic charm through boat tours on the River Dee, contemplating an alternative vantage point of the city.

Consider embarking on evening excursions for a tranquil experience accompanied by captivating sunset panoramas.

5. Strategic Event Attendance:
- **Tip:** Strategically plan your visit by perusing local event calendars to coincide with Chester's various festivities and gatherings. This intentional approach facilitates a more immersive engagement with the city's cultural vibrancy.

6. Prudent Crowd Management:
- **Tip:** Exercise prudence in scheduling visits to popular attractions during the earlier part of the day to circumvent crowded conditions, thereby optimizing your exploration.

7. Footwear Considerations:
- **Tip:** Prioritize the selection of comfortable footwear, particularly if your itinerary involves extensive pedestrian exploration. Chester's cobblestone streets and historical sites may necessitate considerable walking.

8. Adherence to Local Etiquette:
- **Tip:** Embrace local etiquette and the renowned friendliness of Chester's residents. Adhering to polite interactions contributes positively to the overall experiential quality.

9. Weather Apprehension:
- **Tip:** Anticipate and prepare for varying weather conditions by consulting weather forecasts. A pragmatic approach

involves carrying an umbrella or rain jacket, especially pertinent when navigating Chester's typical British weather.

10. Itinerary Flexibility:
- **Tip:** Foster a flexible itinerary, allowing room for serendipitous discoveries. Chester's myriad concealed gems may be unveiled through spontaneous detours, enhancing the unscripted aspects of your visit.

Incorporating these recommendations into your Chester sojourn is poised to augment the overall experiential quality, offering a nuanced and well-informed approach to navigating this historic city.

Health considerations

In anticipation of your visit to Chester, it is advisable to conscientiously consider various health-related facets to ensure a harmonious and gratifying experience:

1. Medical Services Awareness:
- Tip: Acquaint yourself with the locations of medical facilities within Chester, encompassing hospitals, clinics, and pharmacies, to facilitate prompt access in the event of medical exigencies.

2. Comprehensive Travel Insurance:
- **Tip:** Anticipating potential health-related incidents, it is recommended to procure comprehensive travel insurance before embarking on your journey. Ensure that the coverage extends to medical expenses and emergency repatriation.

3. Meteorological Adaptation:
- **Tip:** Given the variability of weather conditions, exercise prudence by dressing suitably, maintaining hydration, and, if necessary, adjusting planned activities based on prevailing weather forecasts.

4. Considerate Footwear Selection:
- **Tip:** Given the presence of cobbled streets and the likelihood of extended walking, opt for comfortable

footwear to mitigate the risk of discomfort or podiatric issues.

5. COVID-19 Precautions:

- **Tip:** Stay abreast of the latest guidelines and regulations pertaining to COVID-19. Adhere scrupulously to recommended safety measures, encompassing the use of masks, adherence to social distancing norms, and compliance with any local restrictions.

6. Prudent Dietary Choices:

- **Tip:** Exercise circumspection in relation to food and water consumption. Opt for reputable dining establishments, partake in bottled water, and ensure the consumption of thoroughly cooked food.

7. Allergies and Dietary Restrictions Disclosure:

- **Tip:** Effectively communicate any allergies or dietary restrictions to restaurant personnel during dining excursions. Chester's diverse culinary scene often accommodates specific dietary preferences.

8. Solar Radiation Protection:

- **Tip:** For outdoor activities, employ protective measures against solar radiation, including the use of sunscreen, hats, and sunglasses, to mitigate the potential impact of prolonged sun exposure.

9. Emergency Contact Documentation:
- **Tip:** Compile a comprehensive list of emergency contact numbers, encompassing local medical services and pertinent embassy or consulate details, to be prepared for unforeseen eventualities.

10. Restorative Practices:
- **Tip:** Prioritize sufficient rest and hydration throughout your explorations. This conscientious approach significantly contributes to overall well-being, particularly in the context of an active travel itinerary.

Cognizant consideration of these health-related parameters ensures a seamless and enriching visit to Chester, affording the opportunity to fully immerse in the city's offerings while concurrently safeguarding one's well-being.

Security and safety

Safeguarding one's security and well-being in the environs of Chester constitutes a paramount consideration. The following discerning recommendations are proffered to cultivate a secure and apprehension-free sojourn:

1. Situational Awareness:
- **Tip:** Cultivate a vigilant awareness of immediate surroundings, exercising heightened caution in crowded or unfamiliar locales to mitigate potential risks.

2. Prudent Valuables Management:
- **Tip:** Exercise diligence in securing valuables, such as passports, currency, and electronic devices. Avail yourself of hotel safes and contemplate the use of anti-theft accessories for added security.

3. Comprehensive Travel Insurance:
- **Tip:** Prudently invest in comprehensive travel insurance that encompasses medical contingencies, trip cancellations, and loss or theft of possessions. Meticulously acquaint yourself with the intricacies of the policy's coverage parameters.

4. Emergency Contact Protocols:
- **Tip:** Compile a dossier of emergency contacts, encompassing local authorities, embassy or consulate details, and the contact information of fellow travelers, to ensure readiness for unforeseen circumstances.

5. Prudence in Public Transport:
- **Tip:** Exercise circumspection in public transportation, particularly regarding pickpocketing risks. Maintain stringent oversight of personal effects and exclusively avail yourself of reputable transportation services.

6. Nocturnal Vigilance:
- **Tip:** Exercise prudence in nocturnal outings, eschewing poorly illuminated or desolate areas. Opt for well-

frequented routes and contemplate group travel during evening hours.

7. Local Consultation:
- **Tip:** Seek counsel from local denizens or lodging personnel for insights into safe locales, potential hazards, and specific precautions germane to the prevailing circumstances.

8. Health and Well-being:
- **Tip:** Prioritize health considerations, including familiarity with local medical facilities and adherence to extant health advisories, particularly in the context of prevalent health concerns.

9. Digital Security:
- **Tip:** Exercise caution in online interactions. Utilize secure Wi-Fi networks, refrain from divulging sensitive information on public platforms, and adopt prudence in online transactions.

10. Communication Protocols:
- **Tip:** Establish a well-defined communication plan with travel companions, encompassing rendezvous points and contact particulars. Maintain connectivity with acquaintances or family, apprising them of your current location.

11. Cultural Acumen:
- Tip: Acquaint yourself with local customs and cultural norms to preempt inadvertent misinterpretations that could impact personal security.

Integration of these safety protocols into one's travel regimen augments the likelihood of a secure and gratifying experience within the precincts of Chester. Proactive engagement and a steadfast commitment to well-being constitute foundational tenets for a discerning traveler.

Attractions places to visit and things to do

Chester boasts a plethora of captivating attractions, each imbued with historical, cultural, or natural significance, contributing to a multifaceted and enriching visitor experience. The following delineates a selection of noteworthy places and activities to consider:

1. Chester Cathedral:

- **Attraction:** Immerse oneself in the historical and architectural grandeur of Chester Cathedral, characterized by its exquisite Gothic design, intricate stained glass, and contemplative cloister.

2. Chester City Walls:

- **Attraction:** Embark on a contemplative promenade along the meticulously preserved Chester City Walls, affording panoramic vistas of the urban landscape and furnishing a distinctive historical vantage point.

3. Chester Zoo:

- **Attraction:** Engage with Chester Zoo, globally acclaimed for its commitment to conservation and its diverse collection of fauna residing in authentically recreated habitats.

4. Grosvenor Museum:

- **Attraction:** Delve into the city's historical narrative at the Grosvenor Museum, featuring exhibitions spanning archaeology, art, and localized history.

5. The Rows:

- **Attraction:** Traverse the Rows, an idiosyncratic medieval shopping precinct distinguished by its dual-tiered galleries, providing an atypical shopping milieu within a backdrop of historical architectural splendor.

6. Chester Castle and Military Museum:

- **Attraction:** Investigate Chester Castle and its Military Museum, an exploration into the city's military chronicles with a particular focus on the Cheshire Regiment.

7. River Dee Cruise:

- **Activity:** Luxuriate in a boat cruise along the River Dee, affording a leisurely and picturesque observation of Chester's urban panorama and its natural environs.

8. Roman Amphitheatre:

- **Attraction:** Explore the Roman Amphitheatre, a vestige of the city's Roman legacy, showcasing well-conserved remnants of an ancient arena.

9. Storyhouse:
- **Attraction:** Immerse oneself in cultural pursuits at Storyhouse, a contemporary venue hosting theatrical performances, cinematic exhibitions, and literary events.

10. Eastgate and Eastgate Clock:
- **Attraction:** Admire the Eastgate Clock, an iconic timepiece situated above the Eastgate, a historically significant city gateway and a subject of frequent photographic interest.

11. Cheshire Ice Cream Farm:
- **Activity:** Savor a visit to the Cheshire Ice Cream Farm, an indulgent locale not only offering a diverse array of ice cream but also providing recreational areas and farm-centric attractions catering to families.

12. Dewa Roman Experience:
- **Attraction:** Imbibe the Roman legacy at the Dewa Roman Experience, an interactive venue delivering insights into Chester's Roman heritage through engaging exhibits.

This compilation of attractions and activities underscores the city's rich tapestry, catering to a spectrum of interests and ensuring a rewarding and diversified sojourn for every visitor.

Tours and experience in Chester

Chester presents a diverse array of tours and experiential activities designed to cater to a broad spectrum of interests, fostering an immersive exploration of the city's cultural, historical, and scenic dimensions. The following compendium delineates noteworthy tours and experiences that offer a profound engagement with Chester's multifaceted offerings:

1. Guided Walking Tours:
- **Experience:** Undertake guided walking tours led by erudite locals, traversing key landmarks such as Chester Cathedral, the city walls, and The Rows, while unraveling historical narratives and contextualizing architectural significance.

2. Boat Tours on the River Dee:
- **Experience**: Indulge in a leisurely boat tour along the picturesque River Dee, affording a distinctive vantage point for appraising Chester's architectural prowess and its harmonious integration with natural environs.

3. City Walls Tours:
- **Experience:** Participate in specialized tours elucidating the historical import of Chester's meticulously preserved city walls, unraveling narratives about the city's defensive strategies and fortifications.

4. Chester Ghost Tours:

- **Experience:** Delve into the spectral annals of the city with Chester Ghost Tours, nocturnal excursions that interweave narratives of haunted locales, historical enigmas, and encounters with the paranormal.

5. Chester Zoo VIP Experiences:

- **Experience:** Elevate the zoo encounter with VIP experiences at Chester Zoo, entailing behind-the-scenes tours, close interactions with fauna, and personalized guided explorations for an intimate zoological encounter.

6. Roman Tours and Experiences:

- **Experience**: Immerse oneself in Chester's Roman legacy through tailored tours and experiences, exploring archaeological sites, the Roman Amphitheatre, and the interactive Dewa Roman Experience.

7. Chester Beer and Food Tours:

- **Experience:** Indulge in gastronomic delights with beer and food tours, elucidating Chester's culinary landscape, affording samplings of local gastronomy, and uncovering the historical tapestry of venerable pubs.

8. Open-Top Bus Tours:

- **Experience:** Opt for open-top bus tours, providing a panoramic panorama of Chester's landmarks, facilitating the flexibility to alight and explore various attractions at one's own pace.

9. Cruise and Afternoon Tea Experience:
- **Experience:** Merge a scenic boat cruise on the River Dee with an exquisite afternoon tea, permitting the enjoyment of the cityscape from the water while relishing delectable treats.

10. Photography Tours:
- **Experience:** Hone photographic skills with guided photography tours, capturing the quintessence of Chester's architecture, landscapes, and animated street scenes under expert guidance.

11. Arts and Culture Walks:
- **Experience:** Immerse in Chester's artistic and cultural milieu through guided walks exploring creative districts, galleries, and live performance venues such as Storyhouse.

12. Cheshire Countryside Tours:
- **Experience:** Venture beyond the urban confines with tours that traverse the picturesque Cheshire countryside, affording visits to idyllic villages, historical estates, and natural landmarks.

This comprehensive compilation of curated tours and experiential engagements epitomizes Chester's commitment to providing visitors with an enriching and memorable sojourn, marked by profound encounters with the city's diverse and culturally resonant facets.

FAQs

Certainly! Here are some frequently asked questions (FAQs) about Chester:

1. **Q: What is the best time to visit Chester?**
   - **A:** The spring and summer months (May to September) are generally considered the best time to visit Chester when the weather is mild, and outdoor activities are enjoyable.

2. **Q: How can I get to Chester from London?**
   - **A:** Chester is well-connected by train from London. Direct train services run from London Euston, taking approximately two hours. As an alternative, you may go by bus or car.

3. **Q: What are the must-visit attractions in Chester?**
   - A: Key attractions include Chester Cathedral, the city walls, Chester Zoo, The Rows, Roman Amphitheatre, and Eastgate Clock.

4. **Q: Are there guided tours available in Chester?**
   - A: Yes, Chester offers a variety of guided tours, including walking tours, boat tours on the River Dee, ghost tours, and specialized tours focusing on Roman history.

5. **Q: What is unique about The Rows in Chester?**
   - A: The Rows are a distinctive feature of Chester, comprising two levels of medieval shopping galleries with

shops and restaurants. It's a unique and picturesque shopping experience.

6. **Q: Are there family-friendly activities in Chester?**
   - A: Absolutely! Chester Zoo, boat cruises on the River Dee, and family-friendly events at story house are great options for families.

7. **Q: Can I explore Chester on foot?**
   - A: Yes, Chester is a pedestrian-friendly city, and exploring on foot is a fantastic way to discover its charm.

8. **Q: What is the history behind Chester's city walls?**
   - A: Chester's city walls are the most complete Roman and medieval defensive walls in the country. They date back to Roman times and were later expanded in the medieval period.

9. **Q: Are there any annual events or festivals in Chester?**
   - A: Yes, Chester hosts various events and festivals throughout the year, including the Chester Literature Festival, Chester Food and Drink Festival, and the Chester Christmas Market.

10. **Q: What are some budget-friendly accommodations in Chester?**
    - A: Budget-friendly options include chain hotels, bed and breakfast establishments, and budget-friendly inns. Booking in advance often helps secure better rates.

These FAQs provide a starting point for visitors to Chester, offering insights into the city's attractions, transportation, and practical considerations for an enjoyable stay.

Top5 Attraction in Chester

Certainly! Here are five preeminent attractions in Chester, distinguished for their historical eminence and cultural resonance:

1. Chester Cathedral:

- **Elaboration:** Exemplifying the pinnacle of Gothic architectural prowess, Chester Cathedral serves as a nexus of cultural and spiritual significance. Its resplendent interior, adorned with intricate stained glass, beckons exploration into the cathedral's storied past.

2. City Walls and Gates:

- **Elaboration:** Chester lays claim to some of the most meticulously preserved city walls in the British landscape, tracing their origins to the era of Roman antiquity. A perambulation along these bastions affords panoramic vistas of the urban panorama, accentuated by landmarks such as the Eastgate and Northgate.

3. Chester Zoo:

- **Elaboration**: Attaining global acclaim, Chester Zoo stands as an epitome of commitment to wildlife conservation. Its expansive grounds host a diverse array of fauna within naturalistic habitats, delivering an immersive and pedagogically enriching encounter.

4. **The Rows:**
   - **Elaboration:** The Rows constitute a distinctive facet of Chester's architectural heritage, featuring dual tiers of medieval shopping galleries housing an array of boutiques and dining establishments. This architectural marvel bequeaths a shopping experience underscored by historical resonance.

5. **Roman Amphitheatre:**
   - **Elaboration:** The Roman Amphitheatre in Chester stands as an impeccably preserved archaeological site, revealing vestiges of an ancient arena. Visitors are invited to traverse this historical expanse, delving into the annals of Chester's Roman legacy.

This compilation of five paramount attractions encapsulates Chester's profound historical narrative, architectural grandeur, and steadfast dedication to biodiversity conservation, promising visitors an enriching amalgamation of cultural and naturalistic experiences.

Where to eat in Chester

Chester presents a diverse gastronomic landscape, featuring an array of dining establishments that cater to a broad spectrum of tastes and preferences. The following curated list highlights noteworthy venues for culinary exploration:

1. The Chef's Table:

Cuisine: Contemporary European

Elaboration: Renowned for its sophisticated ambiance and inventive culinary offerings, The Chef's Table distinguishes itself through a commitment to utilizing locally sourced ingredients in crafting contemporary European dishes.

2. The Botanist:

Cuisine: British, Pub

Elaboration: Housed in a former library, The Botanist offers a distinctive setting for patrons seeking a diverse culinary experience, featuring an eclectic menu that encompasses hearty British classics and inventive cocktail creations.

3. Hickory's Smokehouse:

Cuisine: American, BBQ

Elaboration: Catering to aficionados of American-style barbecue, Hickory's Smokehouse is a well-regarded establishment, presenting a menu replete with smoked meats, burgers, and a medley of flavourful accompaniments.

4. Sticky Walnut:

Cuisine: Modern European

Elaboration: Acknowledged by the Michelin Guide, Sticky Walnut distinguishes itself through its imaginative culinary repertoire and a commitment to providing patrons with an exceptional dining experience inspired by modern European cuisine.

5. Joseph Benjamin:

Cuisine: British, European

Elaboration: A welcoming culinary enclave, Joseph Benjamin emphasizes seasonal inspiration and locally sourced produce in crafting British and European dishes, fostering a convivial atmosphere.

6. Chez Jules:

Cuisine: French, European

Elaboration: Emanating a charming French bistro ambiance, Chez Jules entices patrons with a menu celebrating classic French fare, complemented by a thoughtfully curated selection of wines.

7. Opera Grill:

 Cuisine: Steakhouse, Grill

 Elaboration: Melding style with substance, Opera Grill stands out as an establishment that combines a sophisticated ambiance with a menu featuring premium steaks, seafood, and a diverse array of grilled specialties.

8. The Architect:

Cuisine: British, Gastropub

Elaboration: Occupying a former architect's office, The Architect invites patrons to savor British gastropub offerings, including burgers, pies, and an assortment of craft beers, all within a distinctive setting.

9. Mad Hatters Tearoom and Bakery:

Cuisine: British, Tea Room

Elaboration: For those seeking a whimsical afternoon tea experience, Mad Hatters Tearoom and Bakery offers a charming venue with a delightful selection of tea blends and delectable pastries.

10. Upstairs at the Grill:

Cuisine: Steakhouse, Grill

Elaboration: Residing in a historic edifice, upstairs at the Grill is renowned for its focus on prime steaks, attentive service, and an ambiance that exudes sophistication.

This assortment of dining establishments in Chester encapsulates a panorama of culinary styles, ensuring a diverse and memorable gastronomic journey for those exploring the city.

Where to shop in Chester

Chester's commercial landscape encompasses a dynamic array of shopping venues, combining established high-street emporiums, bespoke boutiques, and distinctive markets. The following catalogue elucidates recommended locations for retail exploration:

1. The Rows:

Elaboration: The Rows, an antiquated shopping enclave, manifests as a tiered structure housing independent boutiques, artisanal shops, and conventional retailers. Its iconic architectural design renders it a picturesque and historic shopping precinct.

2. Grosvenor Shopping Centre:

Elaboration: Situated centrally, the Grosvenor Shopping Centre accommodates an assortment of prominent high-street brands, fashion outlets, and specialty stores, proffering a contemporary retail experience.

3. Chester Market:

Elaboration: Chester Market, an animated indoor marketplace, offers a diverse array of stalls featuring fresh produce, artisanal wares, and unique commodities, appealing to culinary enthusiasts and those in pursuit of locally crafted goods.

4. Watergate Street:

Elaboration: Watergate Street, adorned with independent establishments, encompasses fashion boutiques, antique purveyors, and eclectic emporiums. It stands as a quaint thoroughfare for unhurried shopping and exploration.

5. Cheshire Oaks Designer Outlet:

Elaboration: Positioned in close proximity to Chester, Cheshire Oaks stands as the largest designer outlet in the UK. It hosts an extensive array of designer and high-street brands, affording discounted selections across fashion, homeware, and more.

6. Bridge Street:

Elaboration: Bridge Street hosts a medley of shops, ranging from nationally recognized brands to indigenous retailers. It constitutes a lively avenue showcasing diverse retail options, encompassing fashion, accessories, and specialty boutiques.

7. Eastgate Street:

Elaboration: Eastgate Street, centrally located, integrates both national chains and local establishments. Positioned in proximity to Chester Cathedral, it provides a spectrum of retail experiences within easy reach.

8. Broughton Shopping Park:

Elaboration: Situated just beyond Chester's confines, Broughton Shopping Park emerges as a retail nexus featuring an array of stores spanning electronics, fashion, and homeware, delivering a comprehensive retail milieu.

9. Northgate Street:

Elaboration: Northgate Street, characterized by a fusion of shops, cafes, and boutiques, emanates a vibrant ambiance. It offers visitors the opportunity to explore an assortment of retail offerings while immersing themselves in the city's distinctive character.

10. Bellis Brothers Farm Shop and Garden Centre:

Elaboration: For a distinctive retail encounter, Bellis Brothers combines a farm shop and garden center. Patrons can procure fresh produce, plants, and gardening requisites within a picturesque setting.

This compilation of shopping destinations caters to diverse preferences, ensuring that visitors can engage in a multifaceted exploration of retail offerings while relishing the unique allure of Chester.

Chester travel final thought

In summation, a visit to Chester unfolds as a multifaceted odyssey, seamlessly intermingling epochs of historical eminence, cultural profundity, and contemporary vibrancy. The indelible architectural legacy encapsulated by landmarks such as Chester Cathedral and the meticulously preserved city walls converges with the picturesque charm inherent in The Rows and the spirited dynamism of the city's diverse shopping enclaves.

Delving into Chester's Roman antiquity, exemplified notably by the immaculate Roman Amphitheatre, alongside immersive forays into the rich biodiversity preserved at Chester Zoo, attests to the city's dedicated custodianship of its historical patrimony and its commitment to sustainable stewardship.

The gastronomic tableau, spanning the refined epicurean offerings at The Chef's Table to the diverse array proffered at local markets, not only satiates the discerning palate but also mirrors Chester's culinary pluralism. Moreover, meticulously curated itineraries and guided tours furnish a nuanced exploration of the manifold dimensions constituting Chester's narrative tapestry.

Whether one ambulates through its cobblestone thoroughfares, partakes in a leisurely sojourn along the sinuous expanse of the River Dee, or immerses oneself in the vibrant milieu of Chester's artistic and cultural pursuits, the city provides an immersive milieu wherein tradition and contemporaneity harmoniously coalesce.

Upon departing Chester, an enduring impression persists—a resonant amalgamation of historical reverence and contemporary vitality, ensuring that the recollections forged within its storied precincts endure as a testament to an indubitably unforgettable vacation.

Printed in Great Britain
by Amazon